I have a secret, please don't tell!
I cannot find Mom's silver bell!

I looked EVERYWHERE for that pretty bell.
I looked very, very, VERY well.

But I cannot find Mom's silver bell.

I looked on the floor in case it fell.
I looked inside my turtle's shell!

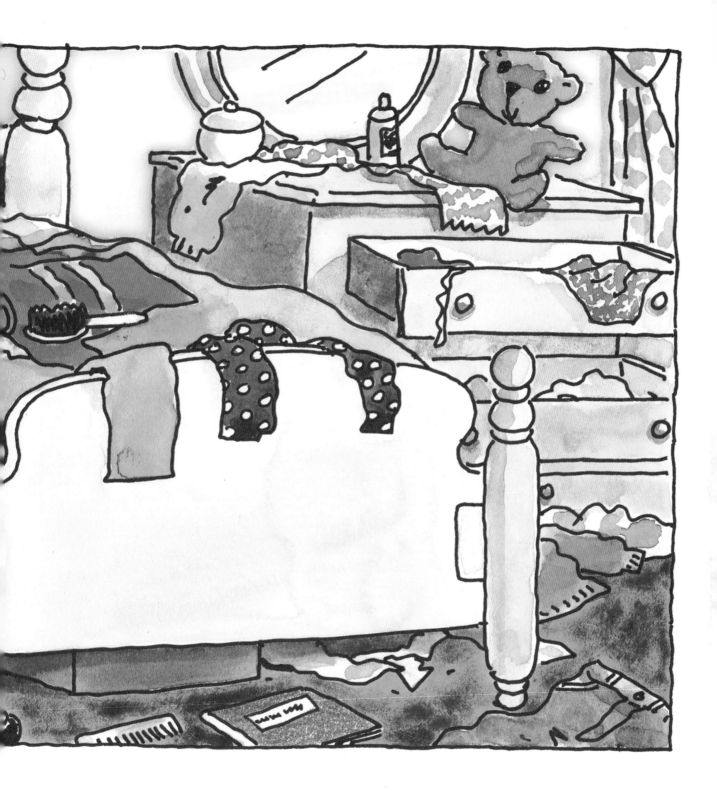

But I cannot find Mom's silver bell.

I even looked where my cat likes to dwell…

6

but I just can't find Mom's silver bell.
Please, oh please, pretty please, don't tell!

Mom really, really, loves that bell.
She always says, "Be careful, Nell."

Oh where, oh where, is that silver bell?

Oh no! That's Mom now! I can tell!

"Hi there, honey.
How's my Nell?"

"Look what I have—my silver bell!
I got it fixed because it fell.
It's as good as new. You can't even tell!"

All this time she had the bell!
Wow, this story turned out swell!

-ell Word Family Riddles

Listen to the riddle sentences. Add the right letter or letters to the -ell sound to finish each one.

1 "Ring-a-ling!" is the sound of the school __ell.

2 I needed a bandage on my knee,
   because I __ell.

3 My turtle is peeking his head out of his ___ell.

4 My nose is the part that helps me to ___ell.

5 In the library you should be quiet.
   You should not __ell.

6 When I had the flu, I did not feel __ell.

7 N-E-L-L is the way you ___ell Nell!

8 Let's open a lemonade stand and __ell lemonade.

9 We're having a surprise party for my dad. Please don't __ell!

10 Another way of saying great is ___ell.

Now make up some new riddle sentences using –ell

-ell Cheer

Give a great holler, a cheer, a yell

For all of the words that we can spell

With an E, L, and L that make the sound –ell,

You'll find it in bell and well and shell.

Three little letters, that's all that we need

To make a whole family of words to read!

Make a list of other –ell words. Then use them in the cheer!